Logos of AMERICAN RESTAURANTS

Taste Tested
by
David E. Carter

Book Design
Suzanna M.W. Brown

Logos of American Restaurants
First published 1997 by Hearst Books International
1350 Avenue of the Americas
New York, NY 10019

ISBN: 0688-15347-X

Distributed in North America by
Watson-Guptill Publications
1515 Broadway
New York, NY 10035
Tel: 800-451-1741
         908-363-4511 in NJ, AK, HI
Fax: 908-363-0338

Distributed throughout the rest of the world by
Hearst Books International
1350 Avenue of the Americas
New York, NY 10019
Tel: 212-261-6770
Fax: 212-261-6795

First published in Germany by:
NIPPAN
Nippon Shuppan Hanbai
Deutschland GmbH
Krefelder Str. 85
D-40549 Düsseldorf
Tel: (0211) 5048089
Fax: (0211) 5049326

ISBN: 3-931884-02-3

Printed in Hong Kong by Everbest Printing Company
through Four Colour Imports, Louisville Kentucky.

Restaurants are everywhere! And new ones are constantly opening. For the graphic designer, this dynamic business represents opportunities to create logos as well as complete identity systems.

This book reflects a cross-section of outstanding restaurant logos from all over the United States. In addition, some menus are shown, as well as one highly detailed example of how a restaurant's visual identity can be expanded into a wide array of items.

I want to extend my thanks to all the design firms who submitted their work for this book. Their willingness to show their outstanding work to the world made this book possible.

David E. Carter
Editor

Restaurant: **Eli's Roadhouse**
Long Island, New York
Creative Firm: **Adkins/Balchunas Design**
Pawtucket, Rhode Island

Restaurant: **Eveready Diner**
Hyde Park, New York
Creative Firm: **Adkins/Balchunas Design**
Pawtucket, Rhode Island

COOL BEANS
CAFE

Restaurant: **Cool Beans Cafe**
Webster Groves, Missouri
Creative Firm: **Phoenix Creative**
St. Louis, Missouri

25 YEARS
PANNIKIN
COFFEE & TEA
COFFEE & TEA
SILVER ANNIVERSARY
SINCE '68

Restaurant: **Pannikin**
San Diego, California
Creative Firm: **Mires Design**
San Diego, California

Restaurant: **Coffee Coffee**
Billings, Montana
Creative Firm: **Advertising Design**
Billings, Montana

Restaurant: **GoJo's**
Billings, Montana
Creative Firm: **Advertising Design**
Billings, Montana

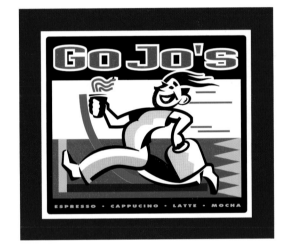

Restaurant: **Stacks The Café**
St. Louis, Missouri
Creative Firm: **CUBE Advertising & Design**
St. Louis, Missouri

MENU

Restaurant: **Harry's Bar & Grill** (menu)
Shorewood, Wisconsin
Creative Firm: **Laura Manthey Design**
Becker Design
Milwaukee, Wisconsin

Restaurant: **Harry's Bar & Grill**
Shorewood, Wisconsin
Creative Firm: **Laura Manthey Design**
Becker Design
Milwaukee, Wisconsin

Restaurant: **The Bay Grill & Bar**
Bozeman, Montana
Creative Firm: **Advertising Design**
Billings, Montana

Restaurant: **Sweet River Grill & Bar**
Merced, California
Creative Firm: **Belyea Design Alliance**
Seattle, Washington

Restaurant: **Edwardo's**

Creative Firm: **Deborah Schneider Design, Inc.**
Chicago, Illinois

"In 1983, when they were three visually disparate restaurants, we designed this logo for Edwardo's Pizza Restaurants. Now their menu is much more than pizza, their locations extend west to Colorado and east to Florida, and the logo developed over 13 years ago still serves them well."

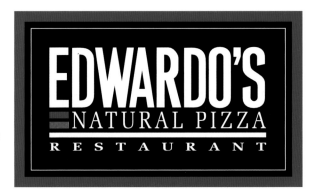

Restaurant: **Pasta Rosa**
Seattle, Washington
Creative Firm: **Belyea Design Alliance**
Seattle, Washington

Restaurant: **Sparta's Pizza and Spaghetti House**
Lynnwood, Washington
Creative Firm: **Hansen Design Company**
Seattle, Washington

Restaurant: **Jake's Steakhouse**
Billings, Montana
Creative Firm: **Advertising Design**
Billings, Montana

Restaurant: **Buffalo Connection**
Birmingham, Alabama
Creative Firm: **DogStar**
Auburn, Alabama

Restaurant: **J. Gilbert's**
Overland Park, Kansas
Creative Firm: **Muller + Company**
Kansas City, Missouri

Restaurant: **Charley's Steakery**
Columbus, Ohio (headquarters)
Creative Firm: **Degnen Associates**
Columbus, Ohio

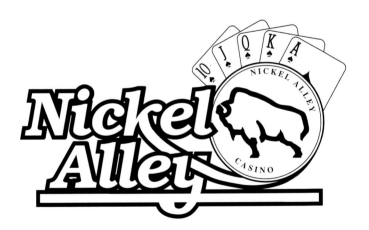

Restaurant: **Nickel Alley**
Billings, Montana
Creative Firm: **Advertising Design**
Billings, Montana

Restaurant: **mick's**

Creative Firm: **Copeland Hirthler
design & communications**
Atlanta, Georgia

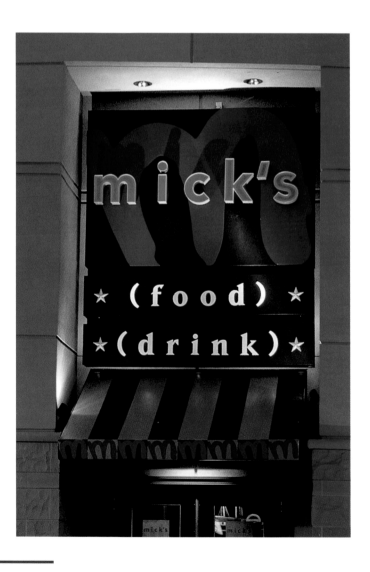

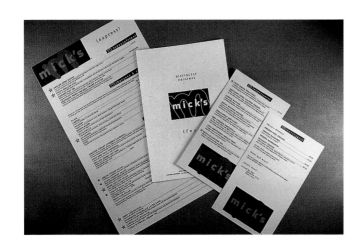

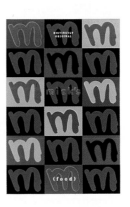

MENU DESIGN

Restaurant: **Eat Smart**
Westwood, Massachusetts
Creative Firm: **Adkins/Balchunas Design**
Pawtucket, Rhode Island

Restaurant: **Westin Hotel & Resorts**
Westin South Coast Plaza
Costa Mesa, California
Creative Firm: **Hansen Design Company**
Seattle, Washington

Restaurant: **Jake's Cafe**
Billings, Montana
Creative Firm: **Advertising Design**
Billings, Montana

Restaurant: **Cafe cafe**
Long Island, New York
Creative Firm: **Steve Trapero Design**
Silver Spring, Maryland

Restaurant: **Mad City Cafe**
Madison, Wisconsin
Creative Firm: **Z•D Studios Inc**
Madison, Wisconsin

Restaurant: **Bagel Works**
Kansas City, Kansas
Creative Firm: **Muller + Company**
Kansas City, Missouri

Restaurant: **Bonjour Bagel Cafe**
Pasadena City, California
Creative Firm: **McNulty & Co.**
Thousand Oaks, California

Restaurant: **Sweet Endings**

Creative Firm: **Cindy Slayton Creative**
Irving, Texas

Restaurant: **Ed's Juice & Java**
Seattle, Washington
Creative Firm: **Belyea Design Alliance**
Seattle, Waashington

Restaurant: **JuiceStop**
Lake Forest, California
Creative Firm: **McNulty & Co.**
Thousand Oaks, California

19

Restaurant: **The Black Forest Cafe & Bistro**
Los Altis, California
Creative Firm: **The Visual Group**
Palo Alto, California

North Shore
BISTRO

Restaurant: **North Shore Bistro**
(menu on facing page)
Milwaukee, Wisconsin
Creative Firm: **Laura Manthey Design**
Milwaukee, Wisconsin

North Shore
BISTRO

Restaurant: **The Deli**
State College, Pennsylvania
Creative Firm: **Sommese Design**
State College, Pennsylvania

Restaurant: **Kosher Market**
Milwaukee, Wisconsin
Creative Firm: **Becker Design**
Milwaukee, Wisconsin

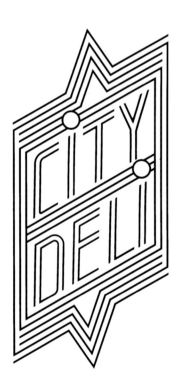

Restaurant: **City Deli**
University Park, Pennsylvania
Creative Firm: **Sommese Design**
State College, Pennsylvania

Second Street Market

Foods for all Seasons

Restaurant: **Second Street Market**

Creative Firm: **McKnight Kurland**
Chicago, Illinois

Restaurant: **The Stadium**
Encino, California
Creative Firm: **The Visual Group**
Palo Alto, California

Restaurant: **River Road Brewery**
Tucson, Arizona
Creative Firm: **Boelts Bros. Associates**
Tucson, Arizona

"River Road Brewery beer logos"

PRICKLY PEAR RED ALE

Iron Pot PORTER

Horned Toad bitter

JAVELINA STOUT

Restaurant: **The Roosevelt Café**
Anchorage, Alaska
Creative Firm: **Kimura Design**
Anchorage, Alaska

Restaurant: **Melina's Breakfast Nook**
Malden, Massachusetts
Creative Firm: **Foscolos Design**
Sudbury, Massachusetts

Restaurant: **Main Street Grind**
New Albany, Indiana
Creative Firm: **Mind's Eye Design Inc.**
New Albany, Indiana

Restaurant: **Stacks'**
Burlingame, California
Creative Firm: **Bruce Yelaska Design**
San Francisco, California

Restaurant: **Eggcellent**

Creative Firm: **Nolin Larosée Design Communications Inc.**
Montréal (Québec), Canada

EUROBISTRO

Restaurant: **Yia Yia's**
(menu on facing page)
Creative Firm: **EAT, Incorporated**
Kansas City, Missouri

Restaurant: **Hugh's New American Bistro**
Denver, Colorado
Creative Firm: **Ellen Bruss Design**
Denver, Colorado

"Silkscreen on stainless."

109 PLAZA STREET
HEALDSBURG
CALIFORNIA 95448
707 433 1380

Restaurant: **Bistro Ralph**
Healdsburg, California
Creative Firm: **Buttitta Design**
Healdsburg, California

29

Ralph — You're the best guy for food + logos — Patti Buttitta

Restaurant: **Brueggers Bagels**
Burlington, Virginia
Creative Firm: **Addison Seefeld and Brew**
San Francisco, California

Restaurant: **La Boulangerie**
Fresno, California
Creative Firm: **Shields Design**
Fresno, California

Restaurant: **Chesapeake Bagel Bakery**
St. Louis, Missouri
Creative Firm: **Kiku Obata & Company**
St. Louis, Missouri

Restaurant: **Le Chic French Bakery**
Miami Beach, Florida
Creative Firm: **Pod New Media**
Coral Gables, Florida

Restaurant: **Cafe Go**
San Francisco, California
Creative Firm: **Bruce Yelaska Design**
San Francisco, California

Restaurant: **Capital Club**
Des Moines, Iowa
Creative Firm: **Sayles Graphic Design**
Des Moines, Iowa

Restaurant: **Riva**
Chicago, Illinois
Creative Firm: **Lipson Alport Glass & Associates**
Northbrook, Illinois

Restaurant: **The St. Petersburg Restaurant**

Creative Firm: **Unit One, Inc.**
Denver, Colorado

Restaurant: **Filiusters**
Westin Hotels & Resorts
Indianapolis, Indiana
Creative Firm: **Hansen Design Company**
Seattle, Washington

Restaurant: **The Landmark Restaurant**
Melrose Hotel
Dallas, Texas
Creative Firm: **Cindy Slayton Creative**
Irving, Texas

Restaurant: **Truett's**
(developed by Chick-fil-Δ)
Creative Firm: **Copeland Hirthler
design + communications**
Δtlanta, Georgia

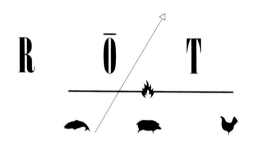

Restaurant: **Rōti**
San Francisco, California
Creative Firm: **Δrias Δssociates**
Palo Δlto, California

Restaurant: **Memphis Roadhouse**
Attleboro, Maine
Creative Firm: **Δdkins/Balchunas Design**
Pawtucket, Rhode Island

MUSEO del JAMON

Caracas, Venezuela

Restaurant: **Museo del Jamón**
Caracas, Venezuela
Creative Firm: **Pod New Media**
Coral Gables, Florida

Restaurant: **Country Pride**
Denver, Pennsylvania
Creative Firm: **Dean Design/Marketing Group, Inc.**
Lancaster, Pennsylvania

Restaurant: **La Rotonda sul mare**
Redwood City, California
Creative Firm: **Bruce Yelaska Design**
San Francisco, California

Restaurant: **Golden Corral**
Raleigh, North Carolina
Creative Firm: **Dennard Creative Inc.**
Dallas, Texas

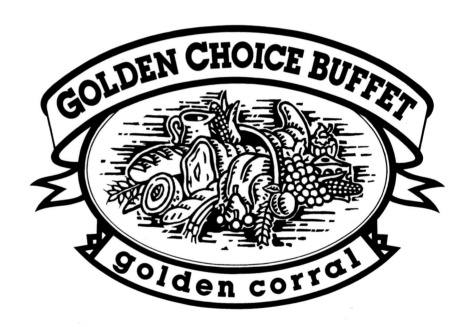

Restaurant: **Golden Corral** (continued)
Raleigh, North Carolina
Creative Firm: **Dennard Creative Inc.**
Dallas, Texas

Restaurant: **Golden Corral** (continued)
Raleigh, North Carolina
Creative Firm: **Dennard Creative Inc.**
Dallas, Texas

Restaurant: **Cafe Bethesda**
Bethesda, Maryland
Creative Firm: **Signal Communications**
Silver Spring, Maryland

e p i c
c a f e

Restaurant: **Epic Cafe**
Tucson, Arizona
Creative Firm: **Boelts Bros. Associates**
Tucson, Arizona

Restaurant: **Otter Lodge**
Rochester, New York
Creative Firm: **South & Hickory Concept & Design**
Rochester, New York

Restaurant: **Russian Bear Restaurant**
San Francisco, California
Creative Firm: **The Visual Group**
Palo Alto, California

Restaurant: **Border Grill**
Indiana
Creative Firm: **Dennard Creative**
Dallas, Texas

Restaurant: **La Piñata**
Burlingame, California
Creative Firm: **Bruce Yelaska Design**
San Francisco, California

Restaurant: **Wabbit Hutch**
Los Angeles, California
Creative Firm: **Steve Trapero Design**
Silver Spring, Maryland

Restaurant: **Apple Creek**

Creative Firm: **Addison Seefeld & Brew**
San Francisco, California

Restaurant: **Picnix**
Billings, Montana
Creative Firm: **Advertising Design**
Billings, Montana

Restaurant: **Little City**
San Francisco, California
Creative Firm: **Bruce Yelaska Design**
San Francisco, California

Restaurant: **Little City**
(Carry Out Section)
San Francisco, California
Creative Firm: **Bruce Yelaska Design**
San Francisco, California

Restaurant: **Great American Food**
San Francisco, California
Creative Firm: **Bruce Yelaska Design**
San Francisco, California

Café **Knickerbocker**

Restaurant: **Café Knickerbocker**
(menu below)
Milwaukee, Wisconsin
Creative Firm: **Becker Design**
Milwaukee, Wisconsin

"On this project we designed a new type treatment to go with the existing mark (Knick Man). We also designed the menus."

Restaurant: **Traffic Cafe**
               St. Louis, Missouri
Creative Firm: **Phoenix Creative**
               St. Louis, Missouri

TRAFFIC
COFFEE **CAFE** CATERING

Restaurant: **Twin Palms**
               Pasadena, California
Creative Firm: **McNulty & Co.**
               Thousand Oaks, California

TWIN PALMS

DIVI RESTAURANT

Restaurant: **Divi Restaurant**
St. Louis, Missouri
Creative Firm: **CUBE Advertising & Design**
St. Louis, Missouri

Restaurant: **Westin Hotels & Resorts**
The Westin Indianapolis
Indianapolis, Indiana
Creative Firm: **Hansen Design Company**
Seattle, Washington

graffitis

Nava

Restaurant: **Nava**
Atlanta, Georgia
Creative Firm: **Antista Fairclough Design**
Atlanta, Georgia

Restaurant: **Todo Wraps**
Seattle, Washington
Creative Firm: **NBBJ Graphic Design**
Seattle, Washington

Restaurant: **Gullifty's**
Elkins Park, Pennsylvania
Creative Firm: **Sommese Design**
State College, Pennsylvania

AT SEATTLE GIFT CENTER

Restaurant: **The Courtyard at the Seattle Gift Center**
Seattle, Washington
Creative Firm: **Art O Mat Design**
Seattle, Washington

Restaurant: **Greenhouse Restaurant**
Corning, New York
Creative Firm: **Michael Orr + Associates, Inc.**
Corning, New York

Restaurant: **Historic Bellefonte Brewery**
Bellefonte, Pennsylvania
Creative Firm: **Sommese Design**
State College, Pennsylvania

Restaurant: **Zinfandels at Sutter Creek**
Sutter Creek, California
Creative Firm: **Scott Brown Design**
Redwood City, California

Restaurant: **Toll House Restaurant & Inn**
Boonville, California
Creative Firm: **Buttitta Design**
Healdsburg, California

PONDEROSA®

Lunch Buffet & Steak Dinners

Restaurant: **Ponderosa**
Metro Media
(logos and
accompanying signs)
Dallas, Texas

Creative Firm: **Dennard Creative, Inc.**
Dallas, Texas

PONDEROSA®

RANCHER'S SKILLET ™

BREAKFAST

B U F F E T

Restaurant: **Ponderosa**
Metro Media
(continued)
Dallas, Texas
Creative Firm: **Dennard Creative, Inc.**
Dallas, Texas

PONDEROSA®

COOK HOUSE ™

L U N C H

B U F F E T

56

PONDEROSA®

STEAK FIXIN'S ™

D I N N E R
B U F F E T

PONDEROSA®

FROSTY BUCKET ™

HOME-MADE TASTE
SUNDAE BAR

Restaurant: **Nino's Steak & Chop House**
(menu, facing page)
Hingham, Massachusetts
Creative Firm: **Adkins/Balchunas Design**
Pawtucket, Rhode Island

Restaurant: **Prego Ristorante**
San Francisco, California
Creative Firm: **Bruce Yelaska Design**
San Francisco, California

Restaurant: **Montrio**

Creative Firm: **Jerry Takigawa Design**
Pacific Grove, California

Restaurant: **Yahooz**
Δ PB&J Restaurant
Kansas City, Missouri
Creative Firm: **EΔT, Incorporated**
Kansas City, Missouri

Restaurant: **Tortilla Factory**
Wichita, Kansas
Creative Firm: **Love Packaging Group**
Wichita, Kansas

Restaurant: **Coyote Grill**
Δ PB&J Restaurant
Mission, Kansas
Creative Firm: **EΔT, Incorporated**
Kansas City, Missouri

Restaurant: **Silverado**
Fresno, California
Creative Firm: **The Visual Group**
Palo Alto, California

Restaurant: **Coyote Grill**
A PB&J Restaurant
Mission, Kansas
Creative Firm: **EAT, Incorporated**
Kansas City, Missouri

Restaurant: **Pentola Taverna**

Creative Firm: **Gregory Thomas Associates**
Santa Monica, California

Restaurant: **Chips**
Ankeny, Iowa
Creative Firm: **Mickelson Design**
Ames, Iowa

Restaurant: **Stars**
(letterhead)
Corning, New York
Creative Firm: **Michael Orr + Associates, Inc.**
Corning, New York

"*an american restaurant*"

STARS

Restaurant: **Mountain Mike's**
Sacramento, California
Creative Firm: **Monnens-Addis Design**
Berkely, California

Restaurant: Garden Grove Food Court

Creative Firm: Copeland Hirthler
design + communications
Atlanta, Georgia

Restaurant: **TropiGrill**

Creative Firm: **Addison Seefeld & Brew**
San Francisco, California

Restaurant: **Peppers Grill & Bar**
Great Falls, Montana
Creative Firm: **Advertising Design**
Billings, Montana

Restaurant: **The Cafe**
Hilton Hotel
Los Angeles, California
Creative Firm: **Arias Associates**
Palo Alto, California

Restaurant: **Hudson Grille**
Los Angeles, California
Creative Firm: **Vince Rini Design**
Montrose, Calfornia

Restaurant: **Taggart's Café & Grill**

Creative Firm: l•earth GRAPHICS

Restaurant: **Bennigan's**
Dallas, Texas
Creative Firm: **Dennard Creative**
Dallas, Texas

Restaurant: **Bennigan's**
(continued)
Dallas, Texas
Creative Firm: **Dennard Creative**
Dallas, Texas

70

Restaurant: **Grand St. Cafe**
Δ **PB&J Restaurant**
(menu on facing page)
Kansas City, Missouri
Creative Firm: **ЄΔT, Incorporated**
Kansas City, Missouri

Restaurant: **Prime Rate Cafe**
Billings, Montana
Creative Firm: **Advertising Design**
Billings, Montana

STEAK & ALE ®

DINNERHOUSE

Restaurant: **Steak & Ale**
S&Δ Restaurant Corporation
Dallas, Texas
Creative Firm: **Dennard Creative**
Dallas, Texas

Restaurant: **La Pêche**
Louisville, Kentucky

Creative Firm: **Walter McCord Graphic Design**
Louisville, Kentucky

Restaurant: **Typhoon Restaurant**
                New York, New York
Creative Firm: **DogStar Design**
                Birmingham, Alabama
                Suka & Friends Design
                New York, New York

Restaurant: **Dante's**
                State College, Pennsylvania
Creative Firm: **Sommese Design**
                State College, Pennsylvania

PERFECT 10 TEN

Restaurant: **Chinsky's Kitchen**
St. Louis, Missouri

Creative Firm: **Kiku Obata & Company**
Stl Louis, Missouri

Restaurant: **Dante's Restaurants Inc.**
State College, Pennsylvania

Creative Firm: **Sommese Design**
State College, Pennsylvania

Restaurant: King Crab Lounge
                  King's Fish House
                  Long Beach, California
Creative Firm: 30sixty design
                  Los Angeles, California

Restaurant: **Belltown Billiards & Restaurants**
Seattle, Washington
Creative Firm: **Art ☉ Mat Design**
Seattle, Washington

Restaurant: **Bar and Books, Limited—The Cigar Bar**
New York, New York
Creative Firm: **Tom Fowler, Inc.**
Stamford, Connecticut

Restaurant: **J.G. Crummer's**
Penfield, New York
Creative Firm: **South & Hickory Concept & Design**
Rochester, New York

THE **SIMON** HOUSE

Restaurant: **Simon House**
(menu on facing page)
Milwaukee, Wisconsin
Creative Firm: **Becker Design**
Milwaukee, Wisconsin

Restaurant: **Landings**
Hilton
Los Angeles, California
Creative Firm: **Arias Associates**
Palo Alto, California

Landings

P e d a l s
C A F E

Restaurant: **Pedals**
Santa Monica, California
Creative Firm: **Arias Associates**
Palo Alto, California

Restaurant: **Healthmex**
Rubios Fish Taco
San Diego, California
Creative Firm: **Mires Design, Inc.**
San Diego, California

Restaurant: **Sweetpea's**
Atlanta, Georgia
Creative Firm: **FRCH Design Worldwide**
Cincinnati, Ohio

Restaurant: **Cafe Espresso at Borders**
San Francisco, California
Creative Firm: **FRCH Design Worldwide**
Cincinnati, Ohio

Restaurant: **Brew HaHa**
The Food Group
Westlake Village, California
Creative Firm: **Mires Design**
San Diego, California

Restaurant: **Paulo & Bill Ristorante**
△ **PB&J Restaurant**
(menu on facing page)
Creative Firm: **E△T, Incorporated**
Kansas City, Missouri

Restaurant: **Alfresco Trattoria**
Santa Barbara, California
Creative Firm: **Jerry Cowart Designers, Inc.**
Woodland Hills, California

Restaurant: **Milano**
Kansas City, Missouri
Creative Firm: **Muller + Company**
Kansas City, Missouri

Casual Northern Italian Dining

TIMBUKTUU™ COFFEE BAR

Restaurant: **Timbuktuu Coffee Bar**
(logos and motifs on facing page)
Des Moines, Iowa
Creative Firm: **Sayles Graphic Design**
Des Moines, Iowa

*"John Sayles designed traditional and monarch-sized
letterhead for Timbuktuu Coffee Bar."*

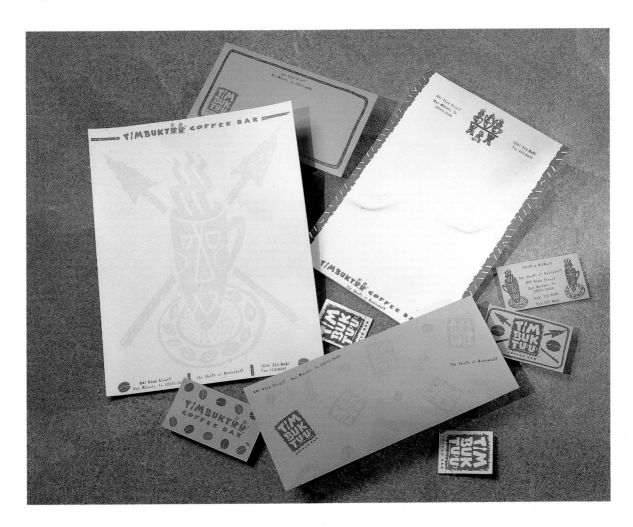

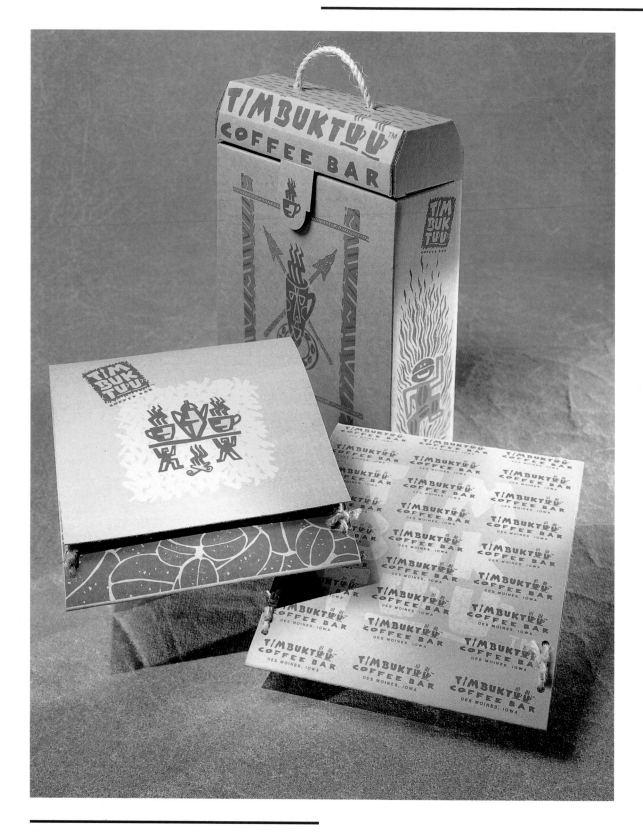

Timbuktuu Coffee Bar
(continued)

facing page
"The opening of Timbuktuu was announced to the local media with this unique and comprehensive media kit."

above
"Timbuktuu's grand opening announcement arrived in a coffee bean bag. Inside whole coffee beans and a wooden stir stick added to the intrigue."

Facing page
*"Coffee beverages at Timbuktuu come in three sizes;
each is presented in a cup designed by Sayles."*

above
*"Pages of the Timbuktuu menu are held in place with
jute twine. The cover is corrugated cardboard."*

Restaurant: **Timbuktuu Coffee Bar**
(continued)

Facing page
"Carry-out and product packaging feature different graphic images."

this page
"BeanΔrt™ is Timbuktuu's private line of artwork and artifacts, for sale to the public as well as used to decorate the restaurant. Shown here are two posters, screenprinted on flat, Kraft paper feedbags."

Facing page
"Timbuktuu's baristas have a choice of neckwear. Both versions are screenprinted on burlap material."

above
"Timbuktuu t-shirts are a hot item at the new coffe bar in Des Moines."

Restaurant: **Timbuktuu Coffee Bar**
                (continued)

Facing page
*"Sayles's involvement in Timbuktuu extended to design
of architectural elements and furniture. Shown here is
the tall table Sayles created from steel and wood."*

above
*"Wooden tabletops feature brightly-painted coffee bean
graphics. The chair backs have a coordinating motif."*

Restaurant: **Timbuktuu Coffee Bar**
                (continued)

*"This is the service area at Timbuktuu. Notice the
product packaging on the counter."*

"Custom-designed tables and uniquely-framed posters are focal points of Timbuktuu Coffee Bar."

"Tall and short tables are perfectly matched to the long interior, divided by spear-shaped railings around a stairway."

"Bright coffee bean graphics are painted on Timbuktuu's wooden tabletops and chair backs. Custom-framed posters complement the look."

Restaurant: **Timbuktuu Coffee Bar**
               (continued)

*"Δ second table style is fashioned from the same wood
and steel as the tall table, but this shorter, bolder figure
'holds' the tabletop above him."*

"Even the steel and wood railings at Timbuktuu Coffee Bar carry motifs."

Restaurant: **Timbuktuu Coffee Bar**
                (continued)

"Sayles designed this mural to be a dramatic focal point of Timbuktuu's interior. Graphic icons and tribal masks are recreated in three-dimensional layers of plaster, then backlit for intrigue."

"The center panel of this exciting three-dimensional plaster mural showcases different graphic icons and the logo of Timbuktuu."

Restaurant: **Timbuktuu Coffee Bar**
                (continued)

Facing page
*"Timbuktuu's clock was hand-built
from a ceramic tile silkscreened
with the coffee bar's logo in
metallic ink."*

above
*"Above the counter, a 24" x 6' corru-
gated cardboard sign is screenprinted
with menu items and prices. 'Order' and
'Pick Up' signs, also screenprinted
corrugated, complement Timbuktuu's
decor and keep counter traffic flowing
smoothly."*

left
*"Guests are beckoned to Timbuktuu by
a sign in the shape of a tree branch,
fabricated from plaster and foam. The
glass storefront gives passers-by a
glimpse into the mysterious interior."*

Restaurant: **Fratelli's of New York**
Geneva, New York
Creative Firm: **In House Graphic Desgn**
Waterloo, New York

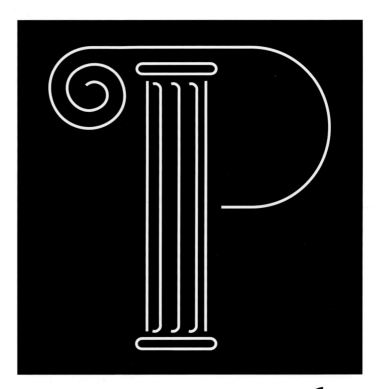

Restaurant: **Pronti's Restaurant**
Geneva, New York
Creative Firm: **In House Graphic Desgn**
Waterloo, New York

Restaurant: **Wine Center**
Corning, New York
Creative Firm: **Michael Orr + Associates, Inc.**
Corning, New York

Baron Steuben Place at Centerway   Corning, New York 14830 · 607·962·6072

SOLANO
CELLARS

WINE SHOP • BISTRO • TASTING BAR

Restaurant: **Solano Cellars**
Albany, California
Creative Firm: **Barrett Communications**
Cambridge, Massachusetts

Restaurant: **Steven Kent Family Restaurant**
            Petersburg, Virginia
Creative Firm: **Smith & Hall**
            Petersburg, Virginia

Restaurant: **Mr. Gatti's**
            Kerrville, Texas
Creative Firm: **Dennard Creative**
            Dallas, Texas

CONTEMPORARY FOODS

Restaurant: **Nancy's Contemporary Foods**

Creative Firm: **McKnight Kurland**
               Chicago, Illinois

Restaurant: **Mr. Gatti's**
               Kerrville, Texas
Creative Firm: **Dennard Creative**
               Dallas, Texas

Restaurant: **Oscar's**
San Diego, California
Creative Firm: **Mires Design**
San Diego, California

Restaurant: **Pacific Street Grill**
Dallas, Texas
Creative Firm: **Dennard Creative**
Dallas, Texas

Restaurant: **Ports cone & grill**
Geneva, New York
Creative Firm: **In House Graphic Design**
Waterloo, New York

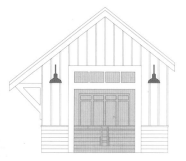

Lakeside, Rt. 14 South, Geneva, NY 789-2020

P   I   C   O

Restaurant: **1 Pico**
Shutters on the Beach Hotel
Santa Monica, California
Creative Firm: **Arias Associates**
Palo Alto, California

Restaurant: **Salsa Rio Grill**
California
Creative Firm: **Dennard Creative**
Dallas, Texas

Restaurant: **Mixology**

Creative Firm: **Love Packaging Group**
Wichita, Kansas

Restaurant: **Now and Zen Restaurant**
Baltimore, Maryland
Creative Firm: **Graves Fowler and Associates**
Silver Spring, Maryland

"A macrobiotic and organic foods restaurant."

Restaurant: **Edibles...Naturally**
Princeton Junction, New Jersey
Creative Firm: **Janet Payne Graphic Design**
Hopewell, New Jersey

Restaurant: **Forge in the Forest**

Creative Firm: **The Wecker Group**
Monterey, California

Restaurant: **erwin**

Creative Firm: **Essex Two Incorporated**
Chicago, Illinois

SEVENTEEN SEVENTEEN

R E S T A U R A N T

Restaurant: **Seventeen Seventeen**
Dallas, Texas
Creative Firm: **David Carter Design**
Dallas, Texas

Restaurant: **Marita's Cantina**
Princeton, New Jersey
Creative Firm: **Janet Payne Graphic Design**
Hopewell, New Jersey

Restaurant: **Star Canyon**
Dallas, Texas
Creative Firm: **David Carter Design**
Dallas, Texas

116

The CALIFORNIA *Grill*

Restaurant: **The California Grill**

Creative Firm: **The Wecker Group**
                Monterey, California

Restaurant: **Chicago Dog and Deli**
                West Des Moines, Iowa
Creative Firm: **Sayles Graphic Design**
                Des Moines, Iowa

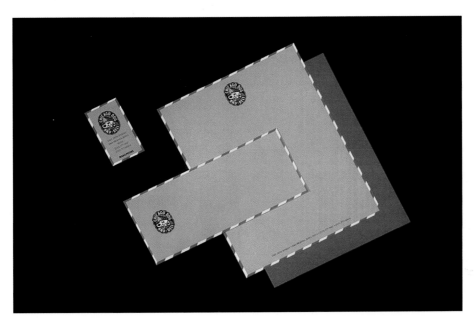

Restaurant: **Rikki Rikki**
Seattle, Washington
Creative Firm: **Hornall Anderson Design Works, Inc.**
Seattle, Washington

Restaurant: **ObaChine**
Los Angeles, California
Creative Firm: **Antista Fairclough Design**
Atlanta, Georgia

ObaChine

ASIAN RESTAURANT AND SATAY BAR

Restaurant: **Big Bowl**

Creative Firm: **Essex Two Incorporated**
Chicago, Illinois

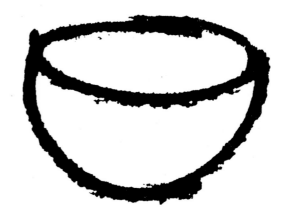

BIG BOWL

Restaurant: **Betelnut**
San Francisco
Creative Firm: **Russell Leong Design**
Palo Alto, California

119

taurant: **Soul Full Cup Coffeehouse**
Corning, New York
ative Firm: **Michael Orr + Associates Incorporated**
Corning, New York

Restaurant: **Jamba Juice**
San Luis Obispo,
California
Creative Firm: **Hornall Anderson
Design Works, Inc.**
Seattle, Washington

Restaurant: **Michael's**

Creative Firm: **The Wecker Group**
Monterey, California

Restaurant: **Panino Presto**
Warwick, Rhode Island
Creative Firm: **Adkins/Balchunas Design**
Pawtucket, Rhode Island

Restaurant: **The Willows**

Creative Firm: **Greenfield/Belser Ltd**
Washington, D.C.

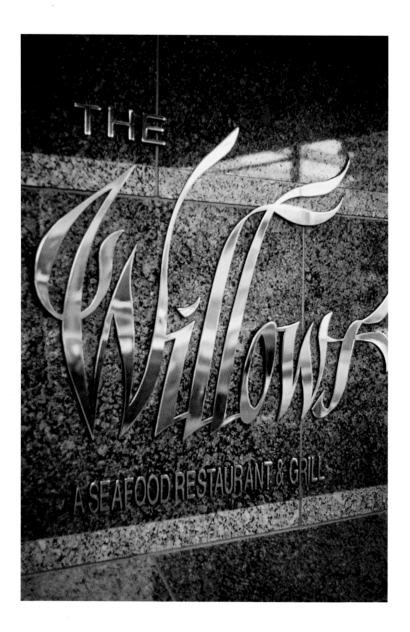

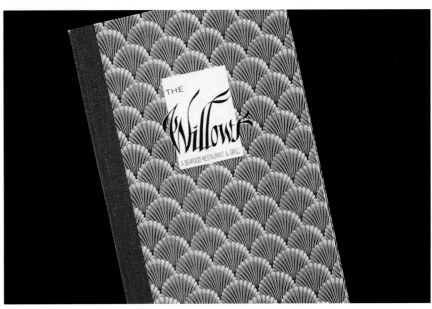

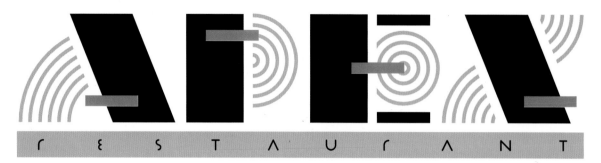

Restaurant: **Apex Restaurant**
Fresno, California
Creative Firm: **Shields Design**
Fresno, California

Restaurant: **The Food Court**
Boston Massachusetts
Creative Firm: **Adkins/Balchunas Design**
Pawtucket, Rhode Island

Restaurant: **Tosca**
Hingham, Massachusetts
Creative Firm: **Adkins/Balchunas Design**
Pawtucket, Rhode Island

Restaurant: **Italia Restaurant**
Seattle, Washington
Creative Firm: **Hornall Anderson Design Works, Inc.**
Seattle, Washington

Restaurant: **Nacho Mamma's**
Des Moines, Iowa
Creative Firm: **Sayles Graphic Design**
Des Moines, Iowa

Restaurant: **The Point**

Creative Firm: **The Wecker Group**
Monterey, California

Restaurant: **Wholé Molé**
Chicago, Illinois
Creative Firm: **David Carter Design**
Dallas, Texas

Restaurant: **Taco Pronto**
New Zealand
Creative Firm: **Mires Design**
San Diego, California

Restaurant: **Munch Market**
Cornell University
Ithaca, New York

Creative Firm: **Michael Orr + Associates**
Corning, New York

Restaurant: **Cornucopia Community Market**

Creative Firm: **The Wecker Group**
Monterey, California

Restaurant: **The General Store**

Creative Firm: **The Wecker Group**
Monterey, California

Restaurant: **California Market**

Creative Firm: **The Wecker Group**
Monterey, California

Restaurant: **John F's Market•Cafe**

Creative Firm: **Greenfield/Belser Ltd**
Washington, D.C.

Restaurant: **Original Monterey Coffee**

Creative Firm: **The Wecker Group**
Monterey, California

Restaurant: **Café Au Lait**

Creative Firm: **The Wecker Group**
Monterey, California

Café Au Lait

coffee specialties and gourmet dishes
carmel-by-the-sea, california

Restaurant: **The Coffee House**
Disneyland
Anaheim, California
Creative Firm: **Evenson Design Group**
Culver City, California

Restaurant: **Peter B's BrewPub**

Creative Firm: **The Wecker Group**
Monterey, California

Restaurant: **Conrad's**
Huntington, New York
Creative Firm: **Adkins/Balchunas Design**
Pawtucket, Rhode Island

Restaurant: **Harry's Bar**
Los Angeles, California
Creative Firm: **Mike Salisbury Communications, Inc.**
Torrance, California

Restaurant: **Timothy's**
Louisville, Kentucky
Creative Firm: **Walter McCord Graphic Design**
Louisville, Kentucky

Restaurant: **Pelican Pizza**

Creative Firm: **The Wecker Group**
Monterey, California

PELICAN PIZZA

Restaurant: **Baldini's**
Boston, Massachusetts
Creative Firm: **Adkins/Balchunas Design**
Pawtucket, Rhode Island

Restaurant: **Time to Eat Pizzeria**

Creative Firm: **Essex Two Incorporated**
Chicago, Illinois

"This is the trademark for a 1950s New York style pizzeria for Lettuce Entertain You Enterprises."

Restaurant: **Double Quick Pizza**

Creative Firm: **The Wecker Group**
Monterey, California

Restaurant: **Spado's**

Creative Firm: **The Wecker Group**
Monterey, California

Spado's
A RESTAURANT

BÄCKERIE
A BAVARIAN BAKERY & CAFE

Restaurant: **Bäckerie**

Creative Firm: **The Wecker Group**
Monterey, California

Restaurant: **Alki Bakery**
Seattle, Washington
Creative Firm: **Hornall Anderson Design Works, Inc.**
Seattle, Washington

Restaurant: **Warburton's**
Chicago, Illinois
Creative Firm: **Δdkins/Balchunas Design**
Pawtucket, Rhode Island

Restaurant: **Red's Donuts**

Creative Firm: **The Wecker Group**
Monterey, California

Restaurant: **Teaism**
Washington, D.C.
Creative Firm: **Signal Communications**
Silver Spring, Maryland

142

Restaurant: **Beauregard's Bakery & Cafe**
Corning, New York
Creative Firm: **Michael Orr + Associates**
Corning, New York

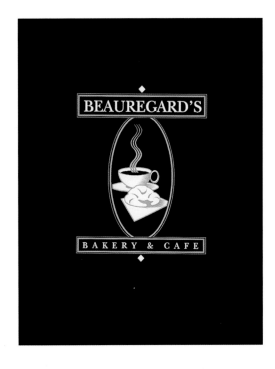

Restaurant: **Bobo's Cafe**
New York, New York
Creative Firm: **Hothouse Designs, Inc.**
Ossining, New York

ACETO CLASSICO

CLASSIC VINEGAR

Bottled & Flavored by Amici
288 South County Road / Palm Beach, Florida 33480
PRODUCT OF ITALY

Restaurant: **Amici Ristorante**
Palm Beach, Florida
Creative Firm: **Elaine Weber Designs, Inc.**
Lake Worth, Florida

AMICI
RISTORANTE & BAR

SUMMER SPECIALS

Enjoy Any

APPETIZER

ENTREE

DESSERT or **WINE***

From our regular menu

PREZZO FISSO $21.00*

MONDAY-THURSDAY 5:30-7PM

BUON APPETITO

~~~~~~~~~~~~

*One glass of wine. Offer valid May 1-September 4. *Plus sales tax & gratuity.

Restaurant: **Amici Ristorante**
(continued)

Restaurant: **Cafe Lulu**
Kansas City, Missouri
Creative Firm: **ЄΔT, Incorporated**
Kansas City, Missouri

Restaurant: **Michael's**

Creative Firm: **The Wecker Group**
Monterey, California

michael's
A RESTAURANT

Restaurant: **Lilly's**
Louisville, Kentucky
Creative Firm: **Walter McCord Graphic Design**
Louisville, Kentucky

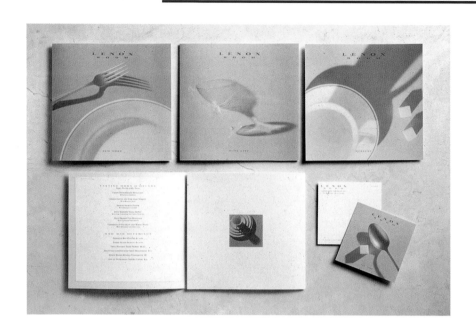

Restaurant: **Lenox Room**
New York, New York
Creative Firm: **AERIAL**
San Francisco, California

Restaurant: **Ladera Restaurante**

Creative Firm: **The Wecker Group**
Monterey, California

Restaurant: **Δ Tasty Affair**

Creative Firm: **The Wecker Group**
Monterey, California

MICHIKO'S GRILL

Restaurant: **Michiko's**

Creative Firm: **The Wecker Group**
Monterey, California

Restaurant: **Union Square Grill**
Seattle, Washington
Creative Firm: **Hornall Anderson Design Works, Inc.**
Seattle, Washington

Restaurant: **Paradise Grill**
Δ PB&J Restaurant
Kansas City, Missouri
Creative Firm: **EΔT, Incorporated**
Kansas City, Missouri

Restaurant: **Paradise Diner**
Δ PB&J Restaurant
Kansas City, Missouri
Creative Firm: **EΔT, Incorporated**
Kansas City, Missouri

Restaurant: **Galaxy Grille**
(menu on facing page)
Palm Beach, Florida
Creative Firm: **Elaine Weber Designs, Inc.**
Lake Worth, Florida

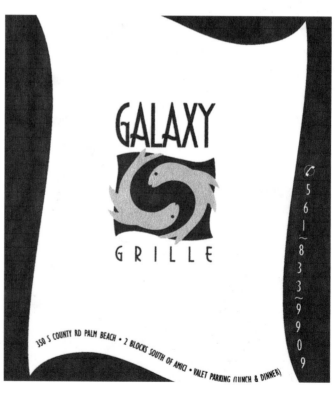

350 S COUNTY RD PALM BEACH • 2 BLOCKS SOUTH OF AMICI • VALET PARKING (LUNCH & DINNER)

Restaurant: **Galaxy Grille**
(continued)

GRILLED JUMBO SHRIMP ON SUGAR CANE SKEWER ~ YELLOW CURRIED RISOTTO

GRILLED SALMON WITH BLACK BEAN SAUCE ~ JAPANESE BROCCOLI FLOWERS, PEAS

WHOLE ROASTED SCORED FISH ~ FIRE ROASTED POBLANO CHILE VINAIGRETTE

CHARCOAL GRILLED SZECHUAN BEEF ~ SAFFRON HOMEFRIED POTATOES

CEVICHE WITH TOMATILLOS ~ CRISPY TORTILLLAS

SIZZLING RICE CAKE ~ ROASTED GOAT CHEESE

WHOLE BROILED LOBSTER ~ TOASTED GRILLED PEARL COUSCOUS

GALAXY
GRILLE

SIZZLING DUCK WITH SPICY MUSHROOM ~ SCALLIONS, ARUGULA, PLUM WINE VINAIGRETTE

SEAFOOD PAELLA WITH SHRIMP, SCALLOPS, PRAWNS, CALAMARI, CLAMS, MUSSELS, WHOLE GRAIN PASTA

GRILLED TUNA WITH BROAD FUN NOODLE ~ SPINACH & CARROTS IN SPICY GINGER CHILE GLAZE

GRILLED SWORDFISH ~ WOK STEAMED VEGETABLES ~ BASIL CHILE BROTH WITH CRISPY NOODLES

350 S COUNTY RD PALM BEACH ~ 2 BLOCKS SOUTH OF AMICI ~ VALET PARKING (LUNCH & DINNER)

561~833~9909

ATOP THE DOUBLETREE

Restaurant: **Brasstree Lounge**

Creative Firm: **The Wecker Group**
Monterey, California

Restaurant: **Jacc's**

Creative Firm: **The Wecker Group**
Monterey, California

Restaurant: **Running Iron Restaurant and Saloon**

Creative Firm: **The Wecker Group**
Monterey, California

Restaurant: **Petrock's**
Belle Mead, New Jersey
Creative Firm: **Janet Payne Graphic Design**
Hopewell, New Jersey

Restaurant: **KnickerBockers**

Creative Firm: **The Wecker Group**
Monterey, California

MORGAN
WINERY

Restaurant: **Morgan Winery**

Creative Firm: **The Wecker Group**
Monterey, California

MORGAN

Restaurant: **Dietrich's**
Louisville, Kentucky
Creative Firm: **Walter McCord Graphic Design**
Louisville, Kentucky

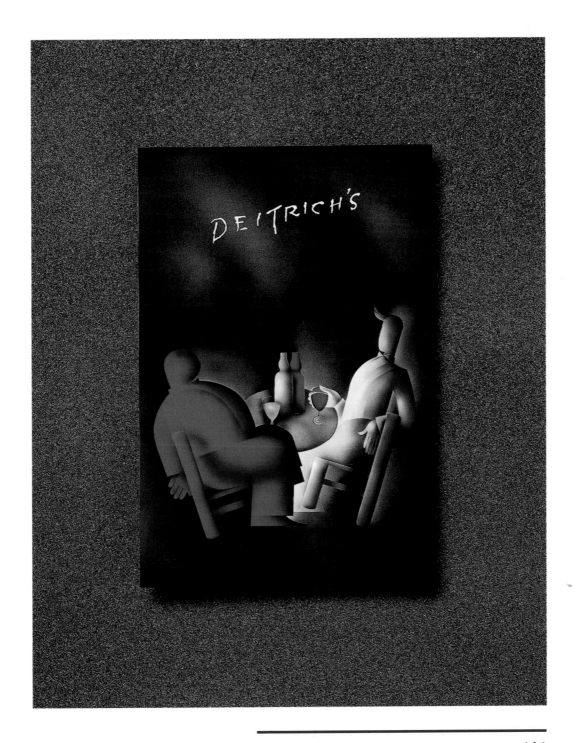

A GASTRONOMICAL EXPERIENCE

Restaurant: **Hammerheads**

Creative Firm: **The Wecker Group**
Monterey, California

Restaurant: **San Simeon Restaurant**

Creative Firm: **The Wecker Group**
Monterey, California

San Simeon Restaurant

Restaurant: **Old Fisherman's Grotto**

Creative Firm: **The Wecker Group**
Monterey, California

Restaurant: **Old Bath House Restaurant**

Creative Firm: **The Wecker Group**
Monterey, California

OLD BATH HOUSE RESTAURANT

Restaurant: McΔbee Beach Cafe

Creative Firm: **The Wecker Group**
Monterey, California

McABEE BEACH
Cafe

·FOOD
·DRINK
·LIFESTYLE

Restaurant: **Dayton Mall Food Court**
Dayton, Ohio
Creative Firm: **FRCH Design Worldwide**
Cincinnati, Ohio

Restaurant: **Chelsea**
The Westin Chicago
Chicago, Illinois
Creative Firm: **Sayles Graphic Design**
Des Moines, Iowa

Restaurant: **The Buckeye Restaurant**

Creative Firm: **The Wecker Group**
Monterey, California

Restaurant: **Blue Fin**

Creative Firm: **The Wecker Group**
Monterey, California

Restaurant: **Sardine City**

Creative Firm: **The Wecker Group**
Monterey, Calfornia

Restaurant: **Caddyshack Café**

Creative Firm: **The Wecker Group**
Monterey, California

Caddyshack Cafè

Restaurant: **Big Shots Sports Cafe**
Dallas, Texas
Creative Firm: **David Carter Design**
Dallas, Texas

Restaurant: **Allo Spiedo**
Louisville, Kentucky
Creative Firm: **Walter McCord Graphic Design**
Louisville, Kentucky

"Allo Spiedo ('on the spit' in Italian) has a kinetic, or multiple identity: the four-color image is the sign and most ads, the other graphics are for the two-color uses (t-shirt, bags, napkins, coasters, etc.)."

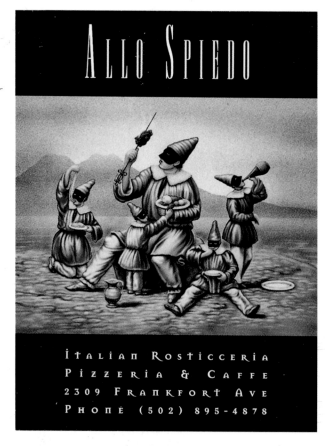

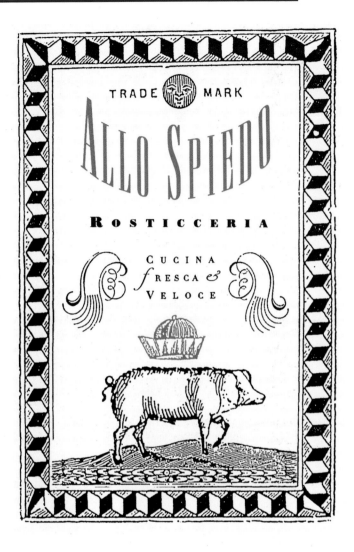

Restaurant: **Mario and Luigi's**
State College, Pennsylvania
Creative Firm: **Sommese Design**
State College. Pennsylvania

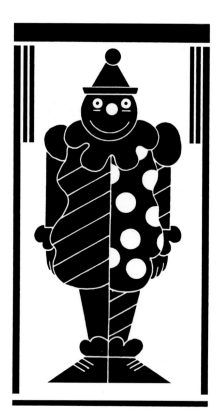

Restaurant: **Mario and Luigi's**
(kids' section)
State College, Pennsylvania
Creative Firm: **Sommese Design**
State College. Pennsylvania

Restaurant: **Gambucci's**
Overland Park, Kansas
Creative Firm: **Muller + Company**
Kansas City, Missouri

Restaurant: **Fratelli's Ristorante**

Creative Firm: **The Wecker Group**
Monterey, California

Restaurant: **Surdi's**

Creative Firm: **The Wecker Group**
Monterey, California

SURDI'S

TWO GUYS *from* ITALY

ITALIAN CUISINE

Restaurant: **The Inn at Hunter's Hollow**
Chagrin Falls, Ohio
Creative Firm: **Herip Design Associates**
Peninsula, Ohio

Restaurant: **801 Steak & Chop House**
Des Moines, Iowa
Creative Firm: **Sayles Graphic Design**
Des Moines, Iowa

Restaurant: **The Inn at Turner's Mill**
Hudson, Ohio
Creative Firm: **Herip Design Associates**
Peninsula, Ohio

CASANOVA
RESTAURANT

Restaurant: **Casanova Restaurant**

Creative Firm: **The Wecker Group**
Monterey, California

Restaurant: **Union Station Brewery**
Providence, Rhode Island
Creative Firm: **Adkins/Balchunas Design**
Pawtucket, Rhode Island

METROPOLIS
rotisseria

Restaurant: **Metropolis Rotisseria**

Creative Firm: **Essex Two Incorporated**
Chicago, Illinois

Restaurant: **Capons Rotisserie Chicken**
Seattle, Washington
Creative Firm: **Hornall Anderson Design Works**
Seattle, Washington

Restaurant: **Taco John's**
Cheyenne, Wyoming
Creative Firm: **Addison Seefeld and Brew**
San Francisco, California

Restaurant: **Cafe Toma**
San Francisco, California
Creative Firm: **Bruce Yelaska Design**
San Francisco, California

Restaurant: **Montana Steak**
Dallas, Texas
Creative Firm: **Addison Seefeld and Brew**
San Francisco, California

Restaurant: **Steamer's Cafe**
Seattle, Washington
Creative Firm: **Hornall Anderson Design Works, Inc.**
Seattle, Washington

Restaurant: **Red Lobster**

Creative Firm: **Lippincott & Margulies**
New York, New York